STEP-UP
SCIENCE

Solids and Liquids

Louise and Richard Spilsbury

Evans

Published by Evans Brothers Limited
2A Portman Mansions
Chiltern Street
London W1U 6NR

© Evans Brothers Limited 2007

Produced for Evans Brothers Limited by
White-Thomson Publishing Ltd,
Bridgewater Business Centre,
210 High Street,
Lewes, East Sussex BN7 2NH

Printed in China by New Era Printing Co. Ltd

Project manager: Harriet Brown

Designer: Flick, Book Design and Graphics

Consultant: Jackie Holderness,
educational consultant and writer.

British Library Cataloguing in Publication Data

Solids and liquids. – (Step-up science)
   1. Solids - Juvenile literature
   2. Liquids - Juvenile literature
   530.4

ISBN-13: 978 0 237 532109

ISBN-10: 0 237 532107

Acknowledgements:

The authors would like to thank Scott Fisher,
teacher at Stokenham Area Primary School for his
invaluable comments and advice on this series.

Picture acknowledgements:

Martyn f. Chillmaid: cover (top left), cover (top
right), pages 4, 4–5, 5, 6, 9b (goggles supplied by
Halfords), 10b, 11t, 12, 14, 15 (all), 17b, 19, 22,
23t, 23c, 23bl, 25, 26t, 27t, 28t, 29. CORBIS: page
21 (Ric Ergenbright). Ecoscene: pages 20b (Eric
Needham), 26b (Sally Morgan). Istockphoto: cover
(main) pages 1, 7t, 7br, 8, 9t, 10t, 13t, 16 (all),
17t, 18 (all), 20t, 23br, 27b, 28b. Photolibrary:
page 24 (Wayne Eastep Photography).

Illustrations by Ian Thompson (pages 7bl, 11b, 12)
and Helen Nelson (pages 13b and 29).

Contents

Looking for solids and liquids

Everything around us is made from different types of material. One way of grouping materials is to say whether they are liquids or solids. These are two states of matter. Look around you now. Which solids and liquids can you see?

Solid materials

Solid materials are used to make many things. The bricks, wood and metal used to build houses and schools are all solid materials. Each of these materials looks very different. Metal is usually shiny and smooth, and bricks are usually red and rough. Other examples of solids are a computer, a ball and a pavement.

How many different solids and liquids can you identify in this picture?

◀ Why do you think we need to use solid materials such as brick, stone and wood to make buildings?

Solids to liquids

Imagine sitting on a sofa that turned into syrup, riding a bike made of runny honey or leaning on a table that suddenly turned into water. Write a funny poem or a news report about how life would be if some of the solids around us turned into liquids.

Liquid materials

Many of the materials around us are liquids or contain liquids. Milk is a liquid that we drink and oil is a liquid used for cooking. Washing-up liquid is useful for cleaning dishes, and shampoo and bubble bath help us get clean in the bath or shower. The most important liquid of all is water. Without water, humans and all the other living things on the planet could not survive.

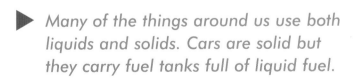

► *Many of the things around us use both liquids and solids. Cars are solid but they carry fuel tanks full of liquid fuel.*

What is a solid?

There are many types of solid substance on Earth. You can easily identify solids because they do not change their shape when left alone.

Solid shapes

Many solids are stiff or hard, such as wood. Other solids are more tricky to spot because they are soft, such as wool or sponge. But we know that these objects are solids because when we put them on a table, they hold their shape.

Sometimes we can change the shape of a solid by applying a force to it. We can change the shape of some solids, such as wood or paper, by cutting them. How could you change the shape of a lump of plasticine?

Can solids flow?

Most solids cannot be poured. They do not flow. Some solids, such as sugar and sand, seem to flow like liquids because they are made from hundreds of very small pieces. Each small piece is a solid and has a fixed shape. When you pour sand, it forms a pile on a flat surface. What do you think would happen to a liquid if you poured it onto a flat surface?

Are all the things in this picture solids? What do they have in common and how do they differ?

Powders such as flour are solids, even though they seem to flow and pour as if they are liquids.

Make a solid model

To make a salt dough model, measure 200 g of plain flour, 100 g of salt and 1 tablespoon of vegetable oil. Put them all into a mixing bowl. Gradually add 200 ml of water and mix well. Knead the mixture with your hands for 10 minutes to get a smooth, soft, solid dough. Press the dough into any shape you like. The soft dough will take two or three days to dry into a hard, solid model.

Inside solids

Every object in the world is made up of lots of very, very tiny particles called atoms. We cannot see them because they are so small. Even a grain of sand is made up of millions of tiny atoms. In a solid, the atoms are held closely and tightly together. That is why each individual solid, such as a brick or a single grain of sand, keeps its shape when left alone.

These solid stones are made from atoms. The atoms are too small for us to see.

▼ The atoms that make up solids are held tightly together.

Using solids

The properties of an object state how it looks, feels or acts. All solids have particular properties. For example, when we say wood is hard and strong, we are talking about its properties. Words like big and small do not describe properties because we can cut solid materials to change their size. Different properties make materials suitable for different uses.

Hard or soft

Some solids are hard but also flexible. Solids that have these properties, such as fibreglass, can be useful for making boat hulls. One of the properties of metal is its ability to become sharp. This is why metal is used for knives and saws. Sometimes we need solids to be soft, such as the feathers that are used to fill cushions and duvets. We need other solids to be stretchy and elastic, such as the fabrics used for socks and swimming costumes. Cling film is also a solid and is made from plastic. What properties does it have that make it good for wrapping food?

◄ What are the properties of this feather?

▼ This bar chart shows the results of a test to find the stretchiest of four fabrics. The four pieces of fabric had weights attached to them to see how far they stretched. Which was the stretchiest fabric? Which fabric stretched the least?

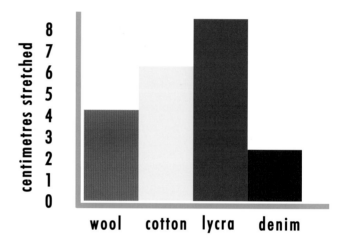

A bar chart to show how far four fabrics stretch

centimetres stretched: 8 7 6 5 4 3 2 1 0

wool   cotton   lycra   denim

Testing the bounce

Balls are made from different materials, such as foam, plastic, leather and rubber. Plan a test to see which solid makes the bounciest ball. Think about how the size of the balls and the height from which you drop them will affect whether or not it is a fair test. Record your results in a bar chart.

Waterproof or absorbent

When droplets of water land on a waterproof solid, they run off the surface. When droplets of water land on an absorbent solid, the water soaks in. Paper towels and bath towels are solid materials that are designed to be absorbent, so we can use them to dry things. If you were designing an umbrella, what properties would the umbrella's materials need to have?

Any sail will catch the wind, but a sail made from a solid that is strong, light, non-stretchy and waterproof gives racing yachts a better chance of winning.

Opaque or transparent

Glass is a solid that is used for windows because it is strong and waterproof. It is also transparent, which means that it lets light pass through it. Some glass needs to let some light through, be strong and waterproof, but prevent people from seeing through it. Frosted glass has these properties. It is translucent, which means that it only allows some light to pass through it. Opaque materials do not allow any light to pass through. This book is opaque.

▲ Goggles and glasses come in different shapes, sizes and colours. One property they must share is transparency.

What is a liquid?

Runny honey, hot chocolate, paints and shampoos are all liquids, but they are all very different. All liquids have features in common that help us to identify them.

Liquids pour and flow

Liquids can flow and be poured. When we turn on a tap or pour a jug of milk, the liquid flows out quickly and smoothly into our glass. Some liquids pour and flow easily, such as water or juice. Other liquids are thicker and flow much more slowly, such as syrup.

Sap is a thick liquid produced by trees. It is so thick that it drips very slowly.

▼ The surface of a liquid is smooth and parallel with the horizon, even when it is poured.

Investigating liquids

Take a spoonful of four liquids, such as water, ketchup, honey and oil. Put a spoonful of each liquid in a line at one end of a metal tray. Try to predict which liquid will reach the other end of the tray first when you tilt it. Next, prop one end of the tray on two books. Which liquid runs down the fastest? Were your predictions correct? How would the experiment be affected if you warmed the liquids on a radiator? What would be the effect of cooling the liquids in the fridge?

Liquids and shape

A liquid does not have a definite shape. Liquids spread out and take the shape of the container they are in. They change their shape when we put them into a new container. The water in a tall, narrow bottle will change shape to fit any container we pour it into. This is also why liquids make a mess if you spill them. The floor has no edges, so spilled liquid goes everywhere. We cannot spill a solid like a book. If we drop it, it still has the same shape.

▶ Spilled liquids like this paint will spread over a wide area.

Inside liquids

The atoms inside a liquid are not as tightly packed and linked together as they are in a solid. They are looser and can move around a little and spread out. This is why a liquid flows and does not hold its shape.

Atom animation

Use the animation at http://www.harcourtschool.com/activity/states_of_matter/ to investigate how the atoms inside solids and liquids are arranged.

▲ The atoms in a liquid are held less tightly than in a solid. They can move around more freely.

World of water

Water is the most important liquid of all. All living things need water, including plants, people and other animals. Without water there would be no life on planet Earth.

Water and us

More than two-thirds of our body weight is made up of water. Most of us could live for a few weeks without food. We would only last a few days without water before our body parts would begin to dry up and die. We should all drink between six and eight glasses (1 litre) of water or non-sugary liquid every day to keep our bodies working properly.

▲ We drink liquids to replace water lost from body processes such as sweating and urination. How many glasses of water or non-sugary drinks do you consume each day?

Plants and water

Plants also rely on water for life. They use it to make their own food. Almost every food chain in the world starts with plants because plants

The world's water

Water covers more than 70 per cent of the Earth's surface, but most of this is seawater. Less than 3 per cent of Earth's water is fresh water. In some parts of the world there is not enough drinking water because the climate is too dry and the people do not have enough money to obtain fresh water.

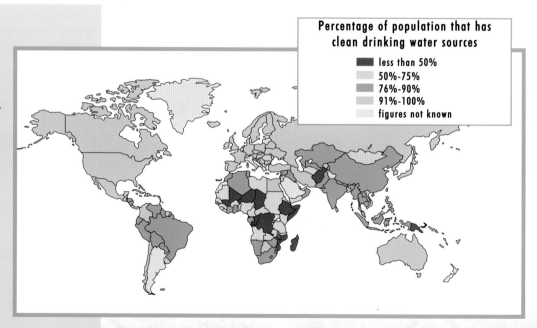

Percentage of population that has clean drinking water sources

- less than 50%
- 50%-75%
- 76%-90%
- 91%-100%
- figures not known

Investigating plants

Prepare two pots with a similar plant in each pot. Predict what you think will happen if one plant only receives salt water and the other only receives fresh water? Plan an experiment to test your predictions. Why would you need two plants? Were your predictions correct?

▲ *Plants need water to live and grow, and we need plants to eat.*

use water, air and sunlight to make food. Our food comes from plants, plant-eating animals and flesh-eating animals, which all need water to drink. Without water, there would be no food for us to eat.

The water cycle

The water cycle is the process by which water circulates from the Earth to the atmosphere (air) and back again. When the Sun heats water at the Earth's surface, some of it evaporates. This means that liquid water turns into water vapour (gas). The water vapour rises. As it does so, it cools and turns back into tiny droplets of liquid water. The droplets group together to form clouds. Eventually, the water falls back to Earth as rain (liquid), hail (solid) or snow (solid), and the cycle begins again.

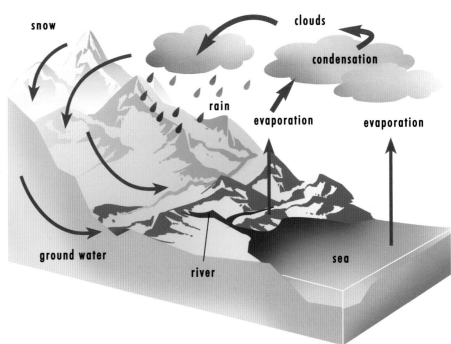

▲ *Use this diagram to describe the water cycle in your own words.*

Measuring liquids and solids

The volume of a liquid does not change unless it evaporates. The volume of a solid does not change unless you break part of it off. This is easy to understand when we think of a solid book, because it does not change its shape. It gets more complicated when we think of a flexible solid such as plasticine. We can change its shape but this does not mean that its volume changes. A liquid takes the shape of its container but its volume does not change.

Liquid volume

We can measure liquid volume using cylinders, measuring cups and spoons. The units most commonly used for volume are litres (l), centilitres (cl) and millilitres (ml). The same volume of liquid can look different depending on the container that it is in. Try it for yourself. Use a measuring jug to measure 125 ml of water. Pour it in turn into different shaped containers, such as a saucer, a bottle and a cup. What shape of container would you choose to make the water level look higher?

▲ Which container looks as though it is holding the greatest volume of water? There is actually the same volume of water in each container.

Solid volume

To find the volume of a solid cube, we measure the length, height and width. Then we multiply the three figures together. If we measure the sides in centimetres, the answer will be in cubic centimetres. However, we cannot use a ruler to find the volume of tricky shapes, such as a spoon. Instead, we can put it into water. The volume of water that an object displaces (pushes out of the way) is the same as the volume of the shape. One centilitre (1 cl) of liquid is equal to one cubic centimetre (1 cm^3). If an object is placed in a jug of water, and the water level increases by 10 centilitres, the volume of the object is 10 cubic centimetres.

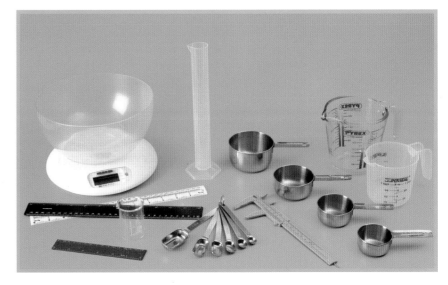

▲ *Which pieces of measuring equipment are used to measure a liquid's volume and which are used to measure a solid's volume?*

Experiment with volume

Make a cube of plasticine. Work out its volume and record your result. Now, re-shape the cube into a long snake. Half fill a cylinder with water and mark the water level. Record this volume. Next, submerge the snake in the water. Measure and record the volume of water again. Which volume will you need to subtract from which to find the snake's volume? How does this compare with the volume that you calculated when the plasticine was a cube?

When an object is placed in water, we can work out its volume by measuring the distance that the water rises.

Can solids become liquids?

When a solid becomes a liquid we say that the state of matter has changed. This happens when the temperature of a substance changes. When a solid is heated, it melts and turns into liquid. When a solid becomes liquid, it is still the same material even though it has changed state.

Melting solids

Different solids melt at different temperatures. The temperature at which a solid melts is called its melting point. For example, an ice cube always melts into liquid water at 0°C, its melting point.

Many solid substances need to be heated before they will melt. For example, butter and chocolate start to melt on hot days or when warmed in a pan.

How do we stop materials such as chocolate, ice or butter from melting? Some materials need more heat than others before they will melt. A wax candle only melts when the candle is lit.

Melting points

Pure substances, such as water, have very exact melting points. Other substances have a range of melting points because they are made from a mixture of ingredients. To make sense of these melting points it may help to know that a hot oven has a temperature of 200°C.

Iron 1,510°C

Gold 1,064°C

Aluminium 660°C

Chocolate 32–36°C

Butter 32–35°C

Ice 0°C

Ice 0°C

Chocolate 32–36°C

Gold 1,064°C

Aluminium 660°C

Iron 1,510°C

Butter 32–35°C

◀ Many scientists say **global warming** *(the general increase in world temperatures)* will melt solid ice at the North and South Poles. How would this change the level of water in the oceans?

Weight change?

When you melt a solid into a liquid it looks very different, but it still weighs the same. None of the substance is lost or gained when it is melted, so there is no change in weight. What test could you do to prove that this is true?

Why do solids melt?

Heat is a form of energy. When a solid is warmed, the heat gives the atoms inside the solid more energy. The extra energy makes the atoms vibrate (move quickly back and forth) more vigorously. At the solid's melting point, the atoms begin to break free from their usual tight arrangement and spread out. This is when the solid becomes runny and turns to liquid.

◀ Chocolate melts between 32 and 36°C. Your body temperature is 37°C. That is why chocolate also melts in your mouth. How could you test whether the size of a piece of chocolate affects its melting time?

Virtual experiments

Experiment with melting points online at http://www.bbc.co.uk/schools/scienceclips/ages/8_9/solid_liquids.shtml

When do liquids become solids?

Liquids become solids when they are cooled or frozen. For example, if we put honey in a fridge for too long it becomes solid and difficult to spread. A solid that has been heated and melted into a liquid will become a solid again when it cools down and hardens.

Changing states

Because you can change a solid into a liquid and then back into a solid, the change of state is described as reversible. It is not a permanent change. However, the substance does not always go back to its original shape. Think about how liquid can be poured into moulds to make solids of different shapes, which is how ice cubes and ice lollies are made.

This liquid lava is hardening into solid rock.

Volcanoes and lava

The centre of the Earth is so hot that the rock there is permanently molten (liquid) and is called magma. When a volcano erupts, the molten rock spurts out. When this happens, the molten rock is called lava. In the air, the lava cools down and hardens into solid rock. Millions of square kilometres of the Earth's surface are formed from cooled lava.

◀ Heat from the Sun melts solid snow into liquid water. Water droplets run downwards, but when they meet the cold air, they freeze into solid ice. As this happens again and again, the droplets build long icicles.

Why liquids freeze

When a substance is cooled, it loses heat energy. This means that the atoms vibrate less and move closer together. By the time the substance is frozen, the atoms have formed a closely packed arrangement. The atoms can hardly move at all. This makes the substance solid.

Why water is special

When most liquids turn into solids they take up less space because the particles bunch together. Water is unusual because when it freezes its particles move apart and it takes up more space. That is why water pipes can split open in winter. In cold weather, drivers add a substance called antifreeze to car water tanks. Antifreeze freezes at a lower temperature than water, which stops the mixture from freezing in the winter weather.

When melted candle wax flows away from the flame it cools and turns back into solid wax.

Icy experiments

Water is unlike many liquids because its volume increases when it becomes a solid. Can you predict what will happen if you completely fill a container with water, put a lid on and then freeze it? How long should you leave the container in the freezer? Try it for yourself – make sure you use a plastic container. Why does the result of this test suggest that we should not put cans of fizzy drink or glass containers in the freezer?

Mixing and separating solids

Think of a mixture of solids such as marbles and beads together in a jar. However hard we try to mix them up by shaking or stirring, we would still be able to pick the mixture apart into its separate solids.

The influence of size

Sand and salt are both made up of similar sized grains. These two solids can be mixed together quite evenly. A mixture of bricks and sand cannot be mixed as evenly. The solids stay quite separate.

Sieving mixtures

Sieves have holes that let small solids through but not larger solids. The hole size that you need depends on the mixture you want to separate. Think about the different hole sizes needed to separate flour and rice, or rice and beans?

Use magnetism to separate solids

The force of magnetism can attract (pull) certain metals towards it. Paper clips are made from steel, a type of metal that can be attracted by magnets (right). Mix paper clips with dry sand. Try using a magnet to separate the paper clips. Could you use magnets to separate coins from sand?

▶ *This magnet is called an electromagnet. It picks up steel waste from a mixture of waste. It leaves aluminium waste where it is because aluminium is not magnetic.*

Density differences

The density of a material is a measure of how heavy a substance is for its size. For example, an iron brick weighs more than a wooden brick of the same size. The iron brick is more dense than the wooden brick. If you dropped them from the same height, the iron brick would hit the ground first because its density is greater.

People can use density to separate materials. For example, wheat grains can be separated from their husks because the husks are less dense than the grains of wheat. The dense grains sink to the bottom, and the husks remain nearer the top.

In some countries, farmers use wind to separate light husks from denser wheat grains. They throw up the grains in the air and the lighter parts blow away. This is called winnowing.

Soil

Soil is a mixture of different sized fragments of rock, parts of dead plants and animals, and water. It forms naturally over a very long time. As you dig a hole in soil, you find larger and larger pieces of rock the deeper you go. This is because the denser pieces sink deepest.

Mixing solids and water

When some solids are mixed with water they seem to disappear, while others sink or float. It all depends on how particles in the liquid and the solid behave with each other.

Making solutions

When some solids, such as sugar, are mixed with water they dissolve. They break into very, very tiny pieces and mix evenly through the water. When a solid dissolves in a liquid, it is said to be soluble. The mixture is called a solution. Tiny pieces of the solid are still there in the water, but they are so small we cannot see them. That is why water looks clear but tastes sweet when sugar is dissolved in it.

▲ Seawater is a solution of salt and water. The pebbles on a beach do not dissolve, so seawater washes over them.

Stirring and solutions

Plan an experiment to find out whether stirring speeds up or slows down sugar dissolving in water. Predict the outcome before you carry out your experiment. How will you time the test and ensure it is fair? How will you display your results?

Making a solution form quickly

Heating a mixture can help it become a solution more quickly. When water is hot, its particles move faster. For example, jelly cubes dissolve more quickly in boiling water than in cold water. Another way of forming a solution more quickly is to use smaller pieces because they dissolve more quickly than bigger pieces. For example, sugar granules dissolve faster than sugar cubes.

Insoluble substances

Solids or liquids that do not dissolve in water are called insoluble substances. Gravel and oil are insoluble. If you put gravel into water it first looks cloudy and mixed, but then the gravel sinks to the bottom. This is because gravel is insoluble and more dense than water. When oil and water are mixed, the oil floats to the surface because it is insoluble and less dense than water.

After mixing gravel, soil and water, insoluble solids settle into layers of different density. The largest and most dense particles form the bottom layer.

◀ Oil is insoluble and floats on vinegar. Before you eat salad dressing, you have to mix oil and vinegar together (bottom image). The oil does not dissolve to form a solution. After a while, the two substances will separate again.

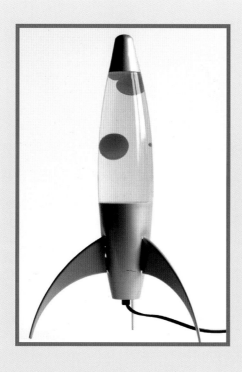

The mystery of the lava lamp

The blobs in a lava lamp are made of a type of insoluble liquid. They float to the top of the lamp when warmed by heat from the base. The heat makes them begin to melt and become less dense than the liquid they are mixed with. At the top, they cool, become more dense and sink again. This keeps the blobs moving mysteriously up and down.

Separating solids from liquids

Insoluble solids usually sink to the bottom or float on the liquid. This makes them easy to separate. Soluble solids are more difficult to separate.

Pouring and skimming

Next time you're at the beach, collect a bucket of sandy water. After a while, you will be able to pour off clear water and leave the sand in the bucket. Solids that float when they are mixed with water can be skimmed off the surface. For example, leaves can easily be collected from an outdoor pool because they float on the surface.

Nets, filters and liquids

Nets are a type of flexible sieve. People use nets to catch fish. The mesh size is the width of the holes in the net. The smaller the mesh size, the smaller the fish you can catch.

A filter is like a very fine sieve. Filters are used in coffee machines. They allow water and very tiny particles of coffee through. They hold back larger coffee particles.

The problem with overfishing

Overfishing is when people catch too many of one type of fish until there are few or none left. When too many small, young fish are caught, they cannot grow up to have their own young and increase the population (total number) of fish. Find out more about overfishing at http://www.ocean-life.info/Overfishing.html. Why do you think some people want fishing-net holes to be bigger?

◀ *A net is a type of sieve used for separating a mixture of solid fish and liquid seawater.*

Can we separate solutions?

Dissolve a teaspoon of sugar into a half cup of water. Then tip it through a clean handkerchief tied so that it covers the top of another glass. Does the water in the second glass taste sweet? The handkerchief can act as a filter for insoluble solids, but when solids dissolve, they break up into such tiny pieces that they even pass through the holes in filters. One way to separate solutions is evaporation. Liquids evaporate when they get warmer because this makes the particles at the surface move faster and faster, until they turn from liquid to gas. People separate salt from seawater by evaporating the water. They collect the salt crystals that are left behind.

Seawater evaporates slowly from shallow pools like this, leaving salt behind.

Everyday materials

Many of the items we use every day are made using the processes of heating and cooling. This turns solids and liquids into new and useful materials.

Metals

When metal is heated, the atoms within it move apart and the metal softens. It can then be stretched to make wire or rolled into flat sheets. The metal sheets can be cut out to make tins. Or they can be cut into sections for vehicle, computer or building parts. When heated to very high temperatures, metal becomes liquid. It can be poured into moulds to make objects like jewellery, saucepans and metal toys. As liquid metal cools, it hardens. The atoms within it squash closely together. This is what makes metal such a strong material.

Paper

To make paper, solid wood is cut into tiny pieces. It is mixed with chemicals and water to make a pulp. This passes along a conveyor belt. The water drains off, leaving damp fibres on the belt. Rollers squash the fibres together to make a mat of wet paper. The mat is heated to evaporate the remaining water and leave a solid layer of paper.

Metals only melt at very high temperatures. How does this make them suitable materials for saucepans and other cookware?

▼ Making paper involves mixing and separating solids from liquids. It also involves heating, cooling and evaporating.

Plastics

Plastic is a very useful solid because it can have different properties. For example, some plastics can be coloured and others are transparent. Plastics can be hard or soft. Hot, melted plastic can be moulded into any shape and when it hardens it stays in its new shape. Plastics are used to make a variety of things such as mobile phones, CDs, trainers and sunglasses. What other plastic items can you think of?

▲ Aluminium metal cans can be recycled. They can be melted down and used again and again.

▼ To make this canoe, plastic grains are stuffed into a mould. The mould is heated so all the plastic grains melt together. When the plastic has cooled, the canoe is taken out of the mould.

Plastics and recycling

Most plastics are made from oil, which is found below the ground. The Earth has a limited amount of oil and once it is used up, it will be gone for ever. This means that oil is a non-renewable resource. Find out more about plastics and recycling on the Internet. How do people cut down on plastic waste? Start your research at http://www.wasteonline.org.uk

Glossary

absorbent   describes a material that soaks up liquid.

atoms   tiny particles from which everything on Earth is made.

climate   weather patterns that happen in a region year after year.

density   the amount of a substance in a certain volume.

displace   to take the place of.

dissolve   to break up a solid into such tiny pieces in a liquid that it seems to have become part of the liquid or even to have disappeared.

energy   property that causes matter to move or change.

evaporate   to change from a liquid into a gas.

filter   a device like a sieve, but with smaller holes that can separate tiny, undissolved solid pieces from a liquid.

flexible   describes something that can bend.

food chain   the living things that eat each other and the order in which this happens.

force   a push or a pull acting upon an object. Magnetism and gravity are types of force.

global warming   an increase in the temperature of the Earth's atmosphere, probably caused by the burning of fossil fuels such as oil and coal.

insoluble   describes a substance that will not dissolve in a liquid.

magnetism   a pulling force that certain metals exert on some other metal objects.

melt   to heat a solid so that it turns into liquid.

melting point   the temperature at which a substance changes from a solid into a liquid.

non-renewable   describes a substance from the Earth of which there is a limited supply and which will run out one day, such as coal, oil or gas.

opaque   describes a material that is not see-through and does not let light pass through it.

particle   an extremely tiny piece of matter.

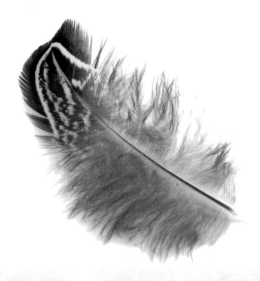

properties the properties of an object describe how it looks, feels and acts.

reversible describes a change that is not permanent.

soluble describes a substance that will dissolve in a liquid.

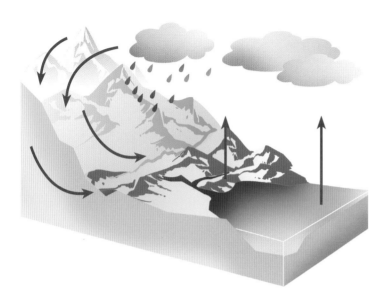

solution a mixture that consists of a substance dissolved in a liquid.

states of matter the different forms in which substances can exist. There are three states of matter – solid, liquid and gas.

substance anything that has mass and occupies space.

temperature a measure of how hot or cold something is.

translucent describes a material that only lets some light pass through it. It is not possible to see objects clearly through translucent materials.

transparent describes a material that is see-through and lets light pass through it.

volume the amount of space that something takes up.

water cycle the process in which water evaporates from rivers, lakes and oceans, rises and turns to tiny water droplets that form clouds, and eventually falls back to Earth as rain, hail, sleet, or snow.

waterproof describes a material that keeps out water.

water vapour water that has evaporated and become a gas.

For teachers and parents

This book is designed to support and extend the learning objectives for Unit 4D of the QCA Science Schemes of Work.

The fact that the world around them is made up of mostly solids or liquids means that this unit helps children understand the relevance and importance of science and technology in everyday life.

Throughout this book and throughout their own investigative work children should be aware that science is based on evidence and they should have the opportunity to:

- Turn questions and ideas into investigations.
- Decide which apparatus to use.
- Predict the outcome of their investigations.
- Understand the need to collect sufficient evidence and conduct a fair test.
- Observe for themselves processes such as melting, dissolving and filtering.
- Use ICT and other methods to record results.
- Work out for themselves what their results mean and how to explain them.

There are opportunities for cross-curricular work in literacy, numeracy, art, design technology and ICT.

SUGGESTED FURTHER ACTIVITIES

Pages 4 – 5 Looking for solids and liquids
Children could try making towers, bridges and tunnels using different solid materials and decide on the best solid materials to use for each structure.

Children could investigate liquids by playing around with a few containers full of liquids of different kinds, to discover for themselves the way, for example, liquids level out when tipped, or the way they can be swirled around.

Pages 6 – 7 What is a solid?
The BBC website has clear information regarding the difference between solids and liquids at the following website: http://www.bbc.co.uk/schools/revisewise/science/materials/08_act.shtml

Pages 8 – 9 Using solids
There is a very useful resource for parents who want to help their children with science at http://www.hep.phys.soton.ac.uk/hycs/ There is a very useful parents' page of information called 'Helping your child with materials' at http://www.hep.phys.soton.ac.uk/hycs/materials.pdf which also has activities and suggestions for everyday situations you can link to science.

Pages 10 – 11 What is a liquid?
The cornstarch experiment ('Is it a solid or a liquid?') is fun and encourages children to think about the definitions of what makes a solid or a liquid. See: http://www.seed.slb.com/en/scictr/lab/cornstarch/index.htm

There is a simple solids, liquids and gases card game to download and print at http://www.collaborativelearning.org/statesofmatter.pdf

Pages 12 – 13 World of water
To help children understand the idea of water vapour, they can investigate whether or not there is really water in the air with activities at http://www.teachtsp.com/products/productextras/SCISCI/watercycle.html Children could make a flow chart to explain how a solid can change into a liquid and into a gas.

Children could research the ways in which people get water in water-poor countries by reading real-life accounts from children at the UNICEF site: http://www.unicef.org/voy/explore/wes/explore_1873.html

Pages 14 – 15 Measuring liquids and solids
Children could have a go at making geometric shapes by cutting out card and glueing sides together to make different solids. Or they could make a chart listing

different solids that can be grouped into different shapes. For example, a can could go in the cylinder column.

Pages 16 – 17 Can solids become liquids?

There is a printable worksheet for children to fill in to help them plan a chocolate melting experiment at http://www.teachingideas.co.uk

Children could follow up on the global warming theme at http://www.climatechallenge.gov.uk/understand.html and perhaps research more about the impact of melting ice on animals such as the polar bear.

Pages 18 – 19 When do liquids become solids?

You could extend this work with a look at mixing plaster of Paris with water to create a solid that is used to help broken bones mend. The difference here is that the water and the particles of plaster of Paris change because they join together, forming a compound, so that they cannot be separated.

Try a drama activity to explain the changes of state between solid, liquid and gas. See: http://www.planet-science.com/sciteach/start.html

Pages 20 – 21 Mixing and separating solids

Children could weigh solids before and after they are mixed to prove that when you mix materials together, the product weighs the same as the sum of the parts.

To continue the soil theme, children could examine a scoop of soil and then put it in a jar of water to settle. They should check after a day or two to see the different layers.

Or, two-thirds fill a jar with a mixture of sand, silt and clay. Add water to fill the jar, shake thoroughly and set aside to settle. This will show the children how the coarser grained solids settle at the bottom, and above that the smaller particles of silt and sand.

Pages 22 – 23 Mixing solids and water

Children could make a mixed vegetable soup and discuss the way this represents all three states of matter – solid vegetables, liquid broth and steam gas. Cooking also helps to reinforce work on measuring solids and liquids.

At http://www.sycd.co.uk/primary/pdf/materials/5.1_dissolving.pdf children learn how to make still lemonade. There is a sheet to fill in that shows the stages in the recipe, with drawings and an activity to reinforce the idea of dissolving.

Children could time how long it takes different solids, such as salt, coffee granules and sugar, to dissolve in liquid and make a line graph with the results.

Pages 24 – 25 Separating solids from liquids

Children could investigate lava lamps. The 'lava' is a solid material that doesn't dissolve in the liquid in the lamp. When heated, the solid becomes less dense and floats to the top, where it cools and sinks again. (You can also uses the lava lamp to help explain convection currents inside the Earth, which links to the volcano information on page 18.)

Children could have a go at making their own salt crystals by following instructions at http://www.planet-science.com/text_only/parents/school_pack/ks2.html

Pages 26 – 27 Everyday materials

Look at some tricky everyday materials to find out whether they are liquid or solid, and how they are made, such as jelly or toothpaste. See the following website for ways to test toothpaste: http://www.wastatelaser.org/resources/toolkits/foss/solid_liquid/lesson15.html

Children could have a go at making their own paper using a paper-making kit from a craft shop or by following the instructions at http://www.recyclezone.org.uk/az_makepaper.aspx The RecycleZone site has lots more information about recycling and other activities such as compost making.

Download a 'fun-size' game at the following website: http://www.sycd.co.uk/can_we_should_we/pdf/explore/fun_size/fun6.pdf This game acts as a revision activity for a series of lessons on states of matter.

Index